Sex, Death and Football

ALISTAIR FINDLAY

Luath Press Limited

EDINBURGH

www.luath.co.uk

First published 2003

The paper used in this book is recyclable. It is made from
low-chlorine pulps produced in a low-energy, low-emission manner
from renewable forests.

The publisher acknowledges subsidy from

 Scottish Arts Council

towards the publication of this book.

Printed and bound by
Creative Print and Design, Ebbw Vale

Typeset in 10.5 point Sabon by
S. Fairgrieve, Edinburgh 0131 658 1763

ALISTAIR FINDLAY has a BA(Hons) in Literature & Social History (Open University), an MA in Applied Social Studies (Bradford University), a Certificate (with distinction) in Scottish Cultural Studies (Edinburgh University) and an M Phil (with distinction) in Modern Poetry (Stirling University). He is the author of *Shale Voices* (Luath Press, 1999), a social-cultural history of the shale oil communities of West Lothian. He lives in Bathgate and works as a Senior Social Worker for West Lothian Council. Other biographical details comprise:

born: 1949 in a miners' row in winchburgh; father: a shale miner, then local journalist, then editor of the west lothian courier; mother: what can you say?; brothers: 4th of 5 sons (was going to be called morag but did not pass the medical); close family: his young brother – morag II – was 10 before he realised his name was not 'bobbyalanjimmyalistairgraeme'; moved to bathgate 1953; family could not go to the coronation because of the flitting; signed for hibs: 1965-8; education: the wee public, the big public, bathgate academy, boni's café, moray house college, bradford university, open university, dundee university, glasgow university, edinburgh university, stirling university, old jock white, bathgate united, big vince halpin, whitburn juniors, pumpherston juniors, bo'ness juniors, fauldhouse juniors, broxburn juniors, nalgo, the communist party of great britain (kidgerie revisionist section), flannigan's singsong, the fairway lounge, boyle's bar (ie. 'the vatican'), the palais, the dreadnought disco, helen, ann, june, jan, jeanette, big tam, wee marion, dan, big eunice, sheila, aunty aggie; takes after: his gran – sarah (kate) cattanach mckinnon

interests: read no poetry between 1970-84, apart from t s eliot – a true modernist despite, or perhaps because of, wearing yon surgical truss

employment history: hibernian fc, golden wonder crisp lorry-loader, apprentice quantity surveyor, clay miner, general labourer, stacker of bricks and big effing roof tiles, builder of reservoirs and scaffolds, social worker since 1973 in falkirk, nottingham, derbyshire, edinburgh, broxburn, livingston

works in progress: an oral-poetical account of scots communism

politics: green-marxist-calvinist-feminist republican

pet hates: the phrase 'nae bother', repeated endlessly, and for no apparent reason, throughout the parish of west lothian

family motto: 'haud the bus'

for all the women in my life, and all the nutters

Acknowledgements

ACKNOWLEDGEMENTS ARE HERE MADE regarding previously published poems: 'Brithers', *Cencrastus*, Autumn issue, 1992; 'Out of History, Gothic Broadcast', *West Coast Magazine*, No 16, 1993; 'The Five Sisters', 'The Steelyard: 1994'; ZED 20, *Akros*, June 1994; 'Fitba' Cliché', 'Jimmy MacGregor's Radio Programme on a Minor War Poet', *Chapman*, Summer, 1995; 'Robert Jamieson of Walls', *Shetland Magazine*, Summer, 1997; 'Game-keepers', HU (formerly *Honest Ulsterman*), No 106, Autumn, 1998.

I thank my brother Graeme for the drawing of John Knox With Walkman intended to accompany 'Gothic Broadcast' (but, unfortunately, lost).

I thank my brother Jimmy for the phrase 'playin like the gress wis oan fire' used in 'Fitba' Cliché'.

I thank my brothers, Bob and Alan, for being my brothers.

I thank Professor Nick Royle, late of Stirling University, now of Sussex University, for the Hamlet/'lobby' reference mentioned in 'The Suitcase in the Attic' – and for writing and editing brilliant, pointy-heidit books such as *Deconstructions* (Palgrave, 2000) and *The Uncanny* (Manchester University Press, 2003).

I thank the Hawthornden Writing Fellowship which allowed me the space and opportunity to complete and edit this collection of poems.

I thank the Scottish Arts Council for funding towards this book.

I thank all the referees who advised the Scottish Arts Council that it was worth the money: Duncan Glen, Vincent Halpin, Alan Jamieson, Joan Johnston, Brendan Kennelly, Mimi Khalvati, Dennis O'Donnell, Rory Watson.

I thank Douglas Dunn for permission to quote some of the final lines of his poem 'The Come-on' in the collection *Barbarians*, published by Faber & Faber, London, 1979.

I thank West Lothian Council, my managers and social work colleagues for their support, and for holding the fort in my absence.

Contents

FOOTBALL

Poet's Preface

Brothers, they say that we have no culture...
One day we will leap down, into the garden,
And open the gate – wide, wide...
And then there will be no wall:
Our grudges will look quaint and terrible.

Douglas Dunn
from *Barbarians*

Sex, Death & Football offers eighteen poems about Sex,
eighteen about Death and eighteen about Football. The title
is a play on the 'literary-critical' notion that all Poetry is
'about' Sex, Death and Poetry. Some of these poems could
well have been placed in other categories or, indeed, in all
of them, which I blame personally on Postmodernism (the
latest radical assault on traditional and settled ways of
thinking, unquote). At one point, I did think of providing
some Notes to accompany these poems so I consulted my
fellow Masons (& Masonettes) in the Craft, only to be
advised by the Chief Shop Steward, a poet of rare eminence
and critical acumen: *jettison them, m'boy; let the bastard
readers do a bit of work themselves for a change.*

So much for Derrida.

Alistair Findlay
Bathgate
April 2003

Foreword

THE FIRST TIME I read Alistair Findlay's poems, they struck me as being full of a Burnsian joy. Reading them again recently, the same exuberance, the same joyous energy and robust delight in being and behaviour came across to me in a way that lifted my heart and stimulated my mind. What we get in Findlay's work is the sort of vitality one finds only in writers whose appetite for life in all its complexity finds expression in a language that seems to wish to embrace that vitality, that appetite, and to share the resulting joy with the reader. This impulse to *share* vision and vitality is at the core of these poems which are both playful and serious, realistic and mythological, disciplined and beautifully wild. This is a smashing book: it smashes through the walls of tedium, boredom, stress and self-obsession that tend to surround life today in so many places. These poems have a liberating, even at times an inspiring effect on the reader. At least, they had on me.

Brendan Kennelly
Dublin

Brendan Kennelly is one of Ireland's most distinguished poets, lecturers and broadcasters. Professor of Modern Literature at Trinity College, University of Dublin, he has over 20 books of poetry published, including *Cromwell, The Book of Judas, Poetry My Arse, The Man Made of Rain* and *Glimpses*. He edited *The Penguin Book of Irish Verse* and his book of critical writings, *Journey into Joy*, is published by Bloodaxe.

Sex

From Scenes Like These

From scenes like these, old Scotia's grandeur springs
Robert Burns
The Cotter's Saturday Night

Big E was that drunk he didn't realise
he was that drunk he'd chatted up the
same bird twice, pulled her, went for
a pee, came back and started talking
to her pal, started talking to her pal.
Meanwhile, Tam's doing his usual, circ-
ling the bar and getting knocked back,
getting knocked back, all night and
sweating like a rapist

Hens-night in a place where squeezing
plooks is as close as you'll get to
foreplay, but the music's great, and
we're all up dancing, when this woman
starts nudging us and telling us to
Fuck Off and Stop Stealin Oor Blokes,
and we're just like smoothing our hair
down and keeping on dancing, and then
she elbows us again

Em has me in her mouth, has me in her
mouth, has me in her mouth, and it's
not even, not even, nine o'clock yet.
The radio comes on, comes on, comes
on, and says it's been a, it's been a
damp start to the day. Em comes on,
comes on, comes on, and she's bursting
the, she's bursting the, she's bursting the
settee

Chunky Chicks: 1966

blood and feathers, blood and feathers, loading bays, overalls, the track, you, packing, dayshift, backshift, nightshift, boredom, cold dawns, twilight zones, yawns, smells, boredom, ribaldry, blood and feathers, wellies, who's fucking who, who you'd like to fuck, who'd like to fuck you, wee Annie – first day in the canteen, everybody there, asking you across the table if you'd like a sook at her tit n then producing this bairn's dummy, fucking red neck, fucking good laugh but, boredom, the ice block, blood and feathers, lorries, going to the pub, going to the Late-night, going to the dogs, going to your work, you, up to your wrists ends in fucking chickens' bums, yes, you pal

Lines on a Toilet Door: 1970

Down the Glen came John Laing's men,
They moved like Fairy Dancers;
One in ten were time-served men,
The rest were Fucking Chancers.

Anon

An Edinburgh firm, building a reservoir in a field up by
        Slammanan; the bus passed
the road end, an 8 o'clock start, and as much overtime as
        you'd want; I joined
a gang draining one end, four feet of mud, shovels, barrows
        and rain, hard graft and
eighty yards long; that's when I first met Geordie McFee,
        Blackrigg, dressed
like a refugee and smoking a roll-up, and only going back
        every third load;
'this'll be the death o' me': work, he meant, no fags, drink,
        or the dogs;
sitting in the hut, slugging tea, he'd tell us about the wife
        and argument;
once, he claimed, after he'd flounced out after some big row,
        his brother entered
the kitchen: 'where's George?', said he, civilly; 'up my arse',
        said she; 'well', said McFee's
brother, 'could ye no take yer knickers aff, for I'd like a
        wee word wi' him?'

Dublin Weekend

I

Dublin. City of Joyce, Ulysses, and the all-day
breakfast, and a photo of Big Eamon with a rubber
Elvis hair-do on. We're in O'Shea Merchants, fifteen
of us, for Eamon's fortieth year, and beer, *yes, that's*
fifteen pints sur, fifteen, yes, fifteen times three. Then
it's off to the Temple Bar, for to chase the Golden Horn.

II

I have lost the power of speech. They have not.
They're half-way round the Horn, eyeing with
deliberate intent, a shoal of girls, from Hull.
One comes aboard without a struggle. They treat
her with respect, call her a goddess, for tomorrow
she will become Deirdre from *Coronation Street.*

III

I am their patient now, being operated on,
but still not out. They do not think I can hear.
They say I am a man to fear, that I could shite
in your ear, and still leave you sleeping. I am
moved, because they move me about. I have no
power of limb. They order me – *mair drink*!

IV

They're doing Sean Connery's all over the bar
– *Mish Moneypenny* – *Jeshush Chroisht!* – O No!
Eamon's got his shirt off! He's getting marriage
proposals from the girls from Hull. He's up on
the bar singing – *Why? Why? Why? Delilah?* His
shirt is a whip. He is farting.

V

A blond woman rises before my eyes: Sorley
MacLean! He'd have called her Colleen of the
Stupendous Thighs. Her pelvis writhes in perfect
time to an Irish jig, her glorious breasts doing
press-ups, up and down, tapping the floor: well,
something's tapping, and it isn't me. She smiles.

VI

I wake. I think I'm in Addiewell. My eyes are like
whippets' balls. I grin. They've taken photographs!
You could land Airdrie on Deirdrie's chin. O Dublin,
City of Joyce, Ulysses, and Big Eamon, City of Colleen,
City of jigging, City of the loin-cloth rising, City of
books, and the all-day breakfast: *beimid ar ais agus aris*
                                                    (we shall return)

The Co-op Hall: 1969

We broke up, nineteen, know, and me a real depressin'
        bastard, no happy wi'
the work, and no going to university, like she did,
        then she leaves
the halls of residence for a flat, and rumours of parties
        I wasn't at,
set in; I go on the bull-run, Saturdays, the West End,
        The Place,
pulling fat birds, The Four Tops booming away, taking
        their tights down
in New Town door-ways, making dates only one of us
        means to keep, the late-bus hame.

Then a Christmas dance, in Bathgate, and she's there,
        bold as brass, dancin'
wi' a wee Edinburgh lawyer, and her pal, Wilma, on a
        weekend pass from Cowdenbeath;
I strode until our noses meet - the first time in yonks –
        'Whit's this?'
'She can do whit she likes. You don't own her.' – thus
        Wilma speaks –
'Well, she can do it somewhere else, and you can fuck off
        back to the piggery.'

Then Tich made a worse mistake, he touched my shoulder,
        so he got
what he came for, a Bathgate *kiss* – it was before I became
        a social worker –
but it was alright, I knew the bouncers, an we got hitched,
        ay, the year after next.

Flannigan's Singsong
(testimony of a waiter)

the swingin sixties
bodyswerved bathgate by the way
though we still staggered through the doors
between the ceilidhs of the dying
and the discos of the fatally wounded
hoping we might meet some others there

besides ourselves
barely remembering trampling T S Eliot
to dust (I was studying him then)
on our way to lusts he merely imagined
the way he imagined us – and was afraid –
like we sometimes frighten ourselves

but cultures come and go
like the british car industry, know,
leaving us, well, products –
but of whose imagination?

Flannigan's: 1968

(the Friday Palais Late-Night roar is in, and revving)

A LITTLE BIT OF SHOOSHNESS PLEASE

(Bob Flannigan's doing his MC chore on the mike,
 like trying to fix the sound-system on the Titanic)

You're serving drinks:

Five Moscow Mules, A Bicardi & Coke,
Three Carlsberg Specials – Two wi' Lime –
an a ride (pause) *hame*

You're being stared
by a diminutive Lulu lookalike
nudging her companions towards
the vicinity of your crotch
and daring you to look away

You hold the gaze:

Fancy a pairty at the Plains?   (she says)
Think Am stupit or Whit?   (christ, you're game)
Zat Yir Name?   (her pal)

Saturdays were for the regulars
and the singers – you could have had your pick
of any three Elvis's – each number, word perfect,
timing, tone and grimace, the lot, an exact copy,
off the production line
we all off came

                  a scotch education
                  british leyland
                  closing time

o happy hour
o mitsubushi
o karioki
o swingin bollocks

o jees take me hame

and

      just afore the weekend bends
    just afore the weekend bends
        just afore the weekend bends

a bhuna burryani an a boak up Davy's lane
the Fish and Chip Emporium

Davy says:
>   *oanie coandiments, sir,*
>   *upoan yir grease?*

fine aesthetic judgements these to make
your eyeballs rolling on the floor
and you say:
>   *Davy, jist the sauce n the saut,*
>   *n Davy, nane o yir pish here, Davy,*
>   *please*

then a taxi to your door and hame
the old man's snoring in his vest
your mother's
>   *Whit?*
>   *The chubb's doon, Naw, Again!*

this is the way the world ends
a bang on a door and a whisper:

>   *is your name Ozymandias?*

no, Chardwhitlow
>   *and your finger?*

bloody sore

[*Chard Whitlow*: Henry Reed's parody of T S Eliot's *Burnt Norton*
– a *whitlow* is an inflamed sore on the finger]

Dancing With Big Eunice

(Falkirk Burgh Social Work: 1973-75)

Dancing with Big Eunice was, I have to say,
a complete knee-trembling experience.
She was a big girl, big and bonnie, big in tights,
and without oany. She had a bum that come
straight doon from her hips and curved roond
like welded sheets of metal on the bowsprits
of the Queen Mary.

She was hairy where she needed to be – oan her heid –
she had ringlets and curls, swirls and swurls, and
her eyes seemed to follow your crotch and wink *Hi*
when you walked by her room. Her own walk went
something like *boom-boom*. During the day she typed up
court reports, made tea for perverts and bad jokes,
smiled at persons who fancied sheep

or wasted the time of the Bog Road police. Eunice never
wasted anybody's time. She painted her eyes blue. Her lips
were red and redder grew the more you looked and the
more she looked at you, till they became like a great big
pouting nipple, or a marble, anyway, something round
and proud that you'd like to chew, or maybe you'd like
to chew you.

    She had power over men, I ken,
                            because they told me.

You know that picture by Beryl Cook, *Ladies Night*,
wi' yon male stripper stretching oot his g-string for these
big dames to take a look, well, Eunice would just have
reached right in and grabbed it, saying – *Look! Some'dy's
broke the wee thing's neck!* O, she had a tongue,
make no mistake, and I'll tell you this, she used it for
mouth-to-mouth no hesitate: that's what Eunice called

a kiss.

Her lips were soft, her breath was sweet,
you were in her grip as her tongue unfurled
inside your cheek, and downward drove
towards your feet – then it turned – and growled,
and upward hurled until it curled around your waist,
looking – no licking – for a label, and then Bang
like an automatic washing machine it started up,
and your y-fronts whanged into double-spin; no half-
loads, no low-heat economic settings here,
just the steady beat of a heavy-duty rinse,
a throbbing pre-wash tumble, and a superb blow-dry,
a non-fast-coloured whirring, a chugg, a sough that
sucked you up and hung you inside-out to die, o my
o my – nobody ever kissed you better, except, perhaps,
Wee Marion – though she'll deny it to this day.

Primal Scream

She says things like she's away to get her chakras hoovered,
        like James Herriot,
I suppose, shouts upstairs that he's off to put his arm up
        some cow's arse,
half-way to the oxter, but he'll be back in time for dinner:
        if only
all pain could be so easily reached; she sits with people
        for an hour,
no more, waiting to become this lightening pain conductor:
        they ache,
she hurts, sound nuts, but that's how it works; her and her
        mates
congregate in some parallel universe, seeing auras circling
        round human frames,
like rainbows, or traffic lights going stop, go, get-ready;
        but, I digress;
so, she's driving back from a workshop in Glasgow, the
        singing balls man,
when she feels her ovaries twang: and we both think this a
        good sign.

North Berwick Beach
(for Sheila)

Walking along the west beach from Gullane,
you found a port-hole, rusted, half-buried
in the sand: *I could put a mirror in that
and stick it round with shells.*

You come here a lot, hoping to persuade
passing dogs to stop and play; the wise
ones just increase their pace, warily:
they've people to meet, places to pee.

You nearly wet yourself when my hat blew off
and I ran after it, hells-bells; a jet flew past,
low, a thunderclap overhead: *that's God,
you said, moving his furniture about.*

You pointed to the gull-shit rocks, white-
topped, by Fidra: *that's guano*; you learned
that at school, you thought, 4th year.

We could hear the sea surging in our room,
the east bay, the Bass Rock tilted, a landing
strip for the gods, awaiting day-trippers from
the planet Zogg: they'd send back postcards
saying

      come,
      brilliant,
      brilliant day.

Birniehill Swings

I've a thing here you could stir cold tar wi', Sanny Marr,
      Birniehill swing-park,
summer 1959, during a break in a game of football that
      began at ten in the morning,
and lasted as long as the goalposts did; we were ten
      then, mostly,
Sanny a bit older, maybe fourteen, and his mate, Franny;
      at tea-time,
on beautiful summer evenings, Sanny and Franny stopped off
      on their way
to meet some Falside girls up by Dalling's farm; Franny'd
      leer and rub his

balls in anticipation; those two couldn't play football,
      but what they
didn't know about the human anatomy wasn't worth hearing;
      Sanny specialised in
hard-ons – *I've a thing here ye could steer cauld tar wi'*,
      he'd say,
for lyricism was all in West Lothian; then they'd do their
      Sir Jasper &
The Lovely Maiden Routine – *O Sir Jasper*, Sanny'd coo,
      my mother wont
like it; Franny'd grimace grotesquely: *Your mother's no*
      gettin it!

We'd cheer as they'd saunter off, for they'd be back, with
      tales to tell,
Franny rubbing his balls and licking his lips, or maybe the
      other way round.

Brother Love: 1970s

Mac says: 'he's told me that he loves her, and she's going to
    have his children;
she'll soon be left school, so he'll stay doon here and get
    himself a job, and they'll
move in wi' her mother, tho there's been some problems wi'
    a brother, who loves sheep;
so I've told him the bus is leavin' in two minutes, but he
    says he isnae comin'.

'Mac, ye ken what he's like whenever we cross the Border,
    a romantic at heart;
we've just come doon for Wembley, but I'm sure he'll see
    sense, I'll put it to him
squarely'; and with that, he crossed the road to the lovers'
    nest, put his foot to the
tattie-sacks of his younger brother, and carried him back to
    the bus on his shoulder.

Intergalactic Gargleblast

Who in this Bowling Alley bowld the Sun?

God's Determinations Touching His Elect
Edward Taylor, 1682

You can do anything you want, her
golden hair jiggling, giggling, come
in my mouth, my bum, anything, some
tooth-paste, your bowels will sing,
the ultimate male fantasy she was
offering, and the clincher, a bunny-
boiler she ain't (Glen Close in *Fatal
Attraction*), then Scots Calvinism
kicks in, faced with the unforbidden
fruit, joy, the body's reek, spunk,
come, surplus, runnin doon the street
an oot bye the steps o the St Mary's
Chapel Hall, so ay, it droops

Seeing Off the Ammonites

she
        turning
her words
    not certain
but
        her voice
            a space
to be
                herself
without
                tap tapping
not always
                    her door
but
                she
                    her voice
her granny specs
like glinting steel
like brilliant shields
like Saul
                seeing off

the Ammonites

(and they were no pushovers,
they Ammonites   by the way)

The Senior Social Worker

The senior social worker lives
with a stick of dynamite up his arse
and the words 'clients-complaints-forms'
on a slow-burn towards the powder-kegs
of his balls, while his managers
skulk in their offices like Nazi war-
criminals waiting on phone-calls from
the Institute of Simon Wiesensthal.

He hears his team mutter darkly
in the corridor like the crowds that
gather round the prison-cells of Myra
Hindley, hoping this time she will say:
'Yes, it was me, but now I've found God.'
Well, 'bollocks to that', says the senior
social worker, who would rather have sex with
an air-raid shelter, than neglect his duty

under the Children (Scotland) Act, 1995, to
protect children from public-opinion, press-
gangs, politicians, perverts, piss-poor
parenting, panels, prefects, plook-sookers,
po-faced professionals and persons who drink
polish; the senior social worker is reading
a report: it says a senior police officer had
sex with his own daughter, aged nine, when

his wife became ill, because he was a strong
Christian and did not wish to break his marr-
iage vows by going outside the family; her
vaginal walls are split and she may never
have children of her own; the senior social
worker looks out the window, and growls

Mrs McRobie

Caught sight of Dave McRobie bunking-off school while
      sitting at the
traffic-lights in Graham's Road; saw the beatific face go
      from shock
to delight as his social worker crunched the back-lights of
      a truck that
had moved off, then stopped; the wee bastard tugged at
      his twelve-year old
mate's coat and pointed at me, then run like fuck; Mrs
      McRobie'd say:
'Whit kin ye dae, Mr Findlay?' 'Well, you might open the
      door when I
come up?' 'Ay, right enough.' She had five more, lived on
      fags and beer,
wore a constant peeny, cleaned half the office blocks in
      Falkirk,

morning, noon and night – the Ice-Rink, Sheriff Court, the
      Broo and Polis
Stations, locations not unfamiliar to her clan and crew,
      tho she never
stole a thing in her life, going from office-space to
      office-space
like a coolie changing paddy-fields, and giving her great
      lump of a man
her pay-packets, unopened; 'sair hodden doon', her doctor
      might say,
but she told me herself that Tam, a liar and a thief, in
      the love department,
was a bloody great fuck, but 'whit kin ye dae, Mr Findlay?'
      'Ay, right enough.'
So they put Dave away, and she gret every single day till
      she got him back.

Women With Red Hair

When I was growing up older boys told the younger boys,
      like me,
that women with red hair had teeth inside the thing they
      kept inside their knickers;
my mother had red hair but, you're right, I never did ask
      her where
she kept her teeth; women with red hair were supposed
      to be fiery
and unpredictable, and have names like Betty, or Greta,
      and blood-red
volcanic-ash and sulphur pumping through their veins
      and ate raw-meat,

furiously, though my mother seemed uncommonly fond of
      cheese;
women with red hair had freckles on their arms, and hid
      from the sun
because their skin burnt easily; they washed steps, hung
      blankets out
on the lines to billow and dry, or sat in chairs eating
      Duncan's Hazelnut
Chocolate and bought brown, pure leather gloves from
      Smith's
in Broxburn, and whispered: *don't you tell your faither*
      now, d'ye hear?

Photographs Unsent

[Women are from Venus]	*[Men from Bathgate]*
Did you just come-on tae me the now?	Christ, you've noticed?
Whit aboot my man?	I dinnae fancy him?
Whit if we did somethin' and someone sent photos tae your wife?	I didnae plan tae video the event?
Were you no the wan that said a man and a woman could have a relationship with- oot involving sex?	Ay, but I didnae mean you?
You're a disgrace.	That mean naw?

Porn Star to Beauty Queen

I am not Dirk Thong,
nor was meant to be.

As for the curtain rods,
well, we all make mistakes.

The ankle-bracelets
will be returned
in due course.

The rest I will keep,
the curling-tongs,
the poker.

O Sharleen!

O how we laughed!
– yon wee thing on your shoulder –
one hump or two?

Now we wander the universe
in tears,
      too many wardrobes between us.

I blame your sister.

Death

The Newspaper Man

Your local correspondent is dead. Stop. His circulation stopped when his heart got the news. Stop. His own father's death. Sentence. New para caps. He who wrote the obituaries could not fail to notice an error in the proof – dash – a fatal misprint had smudged him from the mourners' list. Stop. He thought everyone read through the personal columns on the front page. Stop. Apparently not. Stop. Caps on. HE CRIED. Caps off. New Sentence. He who wrote out his life in endless type cried, comma, huge tears rolling down that great stone face like rain down a hoarding space which cried once also I remember for me. Stop. New para. When his only reader died, comma, he rolled himself up and threw himself away. Full stop. Collect charges call 23 lines paid for direct. Stop. Call ends. Stop.

Brithers

When we meet noo thegither,
we nod and say Ay. Ays meet,
then look away, or doon,
silent bearers o' a terrible secret,
we miss him, oor faither.

Withoot lookin, we can see him in
each other's face and voice and hair.
He's there, in that silence between us,
listenin, in that pause, waitin for the moment
when he'll go wi' us for a pint,
oor faither, who lives in oor silence.

Sometimes, he'll sit between us,
listenin tae his stories,
watchin weel kent faces,
scratchin ears, lookin roon or lighin up,
laughin like a pooch at the funny part,
at art and politics and religion, and bloody eejits,
oor faither, comin alive in oor laughter an talk,
reverent only of fitba', poetry and back-breaking work.

We create oorsels as he did, and MacDiarmid,
wi' words and terrible talk and a' the slavers
o' the scottish workin-class, an aristocracy o' havers
pissin wi' the poor against the same bloody wa',
the collective unconsciousness o' a big team ba',
batterin at a' the doors o' the universe
tae see if the cosmos, oor faither, is in –
an gaun tae the gemm.

How they wid laugh tae see, the reduction o' oor history
tae buildin an extension, or worse,
a conservatory!

Ancient footsteps clatter doon echoin stairs,
and eerie memories fa' tae where we whisper here,
thegither, terrible men, makin love in the dark.

Oor mother, waitin till we all come hame,
openin her door on beery breath an singin weans
creatin, an creatin again, that quiet mellow voice
in the hall, oor faither, who sings nae mair.

Out of History

The American tourist looked at me from across
the restaurant table and asked if I was a Low
land Scot and did I still feel enmity towards
the Highlander. I said my ancestors came from
Shetland, Mull, the Black Isles, Berwickshire
and the West, from Glasgow and quite possibly
Ireland, to the Lothians two hundred years ago
where we worked in pits and some of us married
Catholics. I said I nearly signed for Aberdeen
FC when Eddie Turnbull was the manager, and I
bear no grudges.

The Suitcase in the Attic

Never had an attic, and the suitcase stayed under the bed,
    vacant; lofts came
with the colours of the doors in the places we called 'hame',
    and never got opened;
only roof space up there, we supposed, and the water-tank,
    unlagged; no, we kept our things
in the lobby, as in 'loaby', an ex-coal cellar, converted into
    a glory-hole, from the
Latin: 'I glaur'; 'you glaur'; 'he, she or it is manky – bung
    it in there the noo,
for glaur's sake'; then you'd forget about it, till you were
    looking for something else:
football boots, a thing that made jam, a wringer, a brush,
    a broken stretcher, a cobbler's
foot, polish; two bricks for putting the cold-fill wash-tub
    on so's it would reach over
to the sink; wellies; a pile of old *People's Friends*; a Tiger
    Cub motor-bike chain;
a Tilley heater (broke); your school-bag; even Shakespeare
    had one, a loaby, that he kept
Hamlet in (Act IV, Scene III, Line 47), Pollonius, and yon
    dagger; a bayonet from the
First World War; a dog lead on the back of the door, though
    we never kept a dog;
my father's Special Polis baton: Wallace Stevens called them
    palms at the end of the mind,
and they will always be there, waiting, for the people we
    always think we're always going to be.

Game-keepers

My grandfather speaks
(fed up waiting)

Nae Gumption! Nae Gumption!

(here-i-me, three, n
beatin him at draughts)

I can see the green and black squares
the dark wood frame
and him
searching for breath

and soft Borders swears

Sup yer kail, boy! Demned impidence!

We planted things,

me dibblin,

him sayin where

tyin roses up

(the only trellis in the scheme)

Christ man! It's only a fingir!

He stood there,
immaculate

(bonnet, black boots, waistcoat, chain)

before rock and roll
before curiousity

a mystery of string and twine

and clanging deep metallic sounds
and rattles
                    from every pocket

waiting for the *Berwickshire News*.

Every day
a three-cross-Irish
  (3 times 6d)   came
                    and went
                        Tae Demn!

        Look up, boy! Look up!
he'd say
        (he was off Hallelujah folk)

                as his razors flashed

and his collar studs
                    rolled away.

Later, when he died,
I learned that his grandfather,
that had brought him up, had
once been a game-keeper tae.

Gothic Broadcast

the sound of my own roar reaches me from a great distance
Miroslav Holub
The Minotaur's Thoughts on Poetry

from out my mouth
centuries
roar

creatures

rebelling out

and out
and out
and out

ringing

out

all the mediaeval hardmen
of kirk and state

Knox
the Covenanters
the Disrupters
the Papes
the tortured Divines
and Democratic Intellects
defying their daemons
and giving no quarter

and this voice in me

coming with my grandmothers'
dirking the wounded
unreconciled
from Milton to Carlyle
MacDiarmid Gallacher MacLean
and all those terrible
burning men and women
for freedom

and this voice rung out
lunged out more like
blaring in me
a sounding brass song
tongued out
like they do
when they pick up their dead
and run through the streets of Soweto

Robert Jamieson of Walls
(1901-1981)

Robbie Hayknowe,
Robbie K-nowes,
a crofter of Walls.
Dead? O thirteen years since.
He lived with his aunt,
Phyllis, a seamstress.

It seems
            he broke ponies
                        or into a song
delivered the mail
                  when his own fancy took
played the guitar
                 with a finger and thumb,

and murdered *Mary Morison*.

                    He was

lag   a journey of indefinite length
elt   a jumble, bungled work
bass   a fiercely blazing fire

And you,
        are you a Jamieson?

           Ah, your father's cousin, Catherine Tait.

              We wondered what became
              of her (she left in 1878).

My father planned to visit him
to meet before they died
before old Robbie's roof gave in;
they would have laughed a lot
I'm sure.

                    And you
                your roof caved in
            your bedhead rusting in a field
                these thirteen years
            and someone came to ask
                    too late
        would all remember you so well

            and singing Robert Burns?

The Steelyard: 1994
(Bathgate Town Centre)

the car boogies at the lights
juddering the steelyaird
in stereo
a swept back laid back red
coupe sort of ghia type with tyres
and an armadale number plate
pointing out of town
and driven by an eejit
who sells things
at weekend markets
and might have been

in better times

an apprentice at wolfe's
killed in the war
out in twenty-six
a decent centre-half

(an old foundry worker's
 sitting watching this)

christ,
he's only a wean

widnae ken a big ba'
frae a wee yin

they're oor bloody lights but

(then he says)

haw sur
gee tee eff hame
aw right

n get yirself a joab

no his fau't
            the recession
he says – christ, it talks

aye mibbe naw

but yir bongos is bowff aw the same

Previous Cons

'Jimmy, I've a social background report to do on you.'
Tom Wallace, social worker, Falkirk Burgh, 1973

'I don't have a social background, so ye can fuck off.'
Jimmy Dee, who always took the alternative (3 months)

Danny Murphy and his neebs, PC 129 Fat Boab, sat in a
 Panda at the Bog Road lights,
when up creeps a lime-green Ford Capri driven by Fergie
 McLaren McGee, 23 years old
and sallow, a bit like *Huggy Bear*, only darker, no having
 washed for a year and banned
for 30 year concurrent for taking and driving away
 without consent or benefit of clergy,
road tax, insurance, mot, licence plates or mud-guards
 umpteen stolen cars; Fergie
tips his shades, waves, then jumps the lights an hoors it
 South, all the way
to a service-station outside Carlisle, where an attendant
 is left holding,
open-mouthed, a pump spraying petrol out Fergie decides
 not to pay for,
despite having in the backseat the proceeds of a robbery
 in the toon that very day,
then a high-speed chase down the motorway heading for
 Bristol and an ex-Falkirk
enclave, a kind of Hole-in-the-Wall gang, who seem to
 think they can claim,
like John Wayne crossing the Rio Grande, sanctuary from
 a posse and, o ay,
Fergie's on Probation to me, so he gets 2 years 6 months
 consecutive added.

Fergie gets in with some real crooks in Barlinnie and is
      left holding the baby,
10 years straight this time, for re-spraying and re-setting
      cars, his passion,
his legerdemain; Fergie has a wean to Hyacynth McBain,
      an alcoholic,
sometimes insane, 2 days old and being fed Coca-Cola
      when I take the
Place of Safety out; Fergie aye blamed me when she died
      for no acting quicker.

Social Welfare: a Fantasy in Scots

Fellow, you have broken our laws! Yes, your
Honour; but not before your laws had broken me.
William Thom in
Justice Made Easy
Tait's Magazine, Edinburgh, 1857

The gaberlunzie stood
on Waverley Steps,
clinking, wet –

the pennies in her blanket
  jingle

    (they say)

    Ane called Lilley ha'e pished in thir mooths
    – but they've tried a' that afore:

(they mean the Statutes of Perth, 1422-1524)

  Maisters o' Correction sal entertain wasters, sornares,
  overlayers or maisterful thiggers [all types of beggar]
  harbouring on kirkmen or husbandmen [medieval taxpayers]
  an bi a' correction necessar or severe, whipping or other
  wise [excepting torture], jile or cleekit them – gif gear
  enough [if they can pay] – or nail thir lugs til the trone
  [or ony ither tree], or gif retourn, hing them. Coal-
  maisters or Salt-maisters sal enthral ony sich wi siccar
  [similar] powers, for the benefit o' thir wark.

the pennies in her blanket
  jingle

(they say)

>   *An a' this,*
>   *tae redd ye'se frae the camsteerie;*   [rabble]
>   *for the upricht'll dwell in the land,*
>   *and the perfect remain in it,*
>   *but the wicked'll be rutit oot*
>
>   *Ay!*
>   *they'll be rutit oot a' thegither!*
>
>   *Ay!*
>   *Doon!*
>   *Ay!*
>   *And Doon!*
>   *tae the chaumers o' daith*
>
>   *itsel'!*
>   *Ay!*

and we walk past the jingling

                    mouths shut

                                till the rain

The Russian Revolution in Bathgate

On the 60th Anniversary of the October Revolution
the comrades met in the room above the chemist's
(now Haddows) beside the Railway Tavern.

It was Sunday before noon
John Foster's coming through –
fellow-travellers welcome.

The room was bare and wooden,
posters flaking. We all stood,
a minute's silence ticked away,

a half-raised fist, table, chairs,
St David's Church bell tolling
the Bathgate faithful out to pray.

No one laughed, no incongruity here,
twenty-five million war dead,
Foster said, could not be wished away:

we had to win the peace by struggle.
Eric Atkinson handed round some greetings
from some friends we'd found

in Nicaragua.

White-water

She said she was going off to white-water but how would
     she know what I thought
of her, if I didn't say; I laughed, said I'd tell, how she'd
     tried to arrange
her own funeral; *I'm serious*, she said: *What would you*
     say? I said she would
always be, in my heart, that all the bawds of euphony
     would start, and cry,
and I would count them, one, by one, her brilliant days,
     of frost, and sun,
and in the evening, when her poem was done, I'd wait,
     till all the blackbirds had
quietened, and sung: I'd wait, till all the blackbirds had
     quietened, and sung.

Jimmy MacGregor's Radio Programme on a Minor War Poet

Sing me no more sad sounding roundelays
of death and war, of comradeship and gore,
of brotherhood's instinctive reaching to defend
each other until the end, dear friend, no matter
whose, even your own

for this disgrace is a perversion of the deepest trace
memories we own, formed in the midst of every
common birth

clutched and clutching we, gasping for air
through wetness and the blood, gripped
by an overwhelming fear the powerful drive us to,
cracked into life and passed around, clutched
and clutching still, till someone catches hold
and we are held there, fast and sure, unabandoned,
ready to die or kill for that same surety to remain,
over and over again

Wrapt in a Sheet

In the urinals in Bathgate, in the British Legion Club, my
      brother,
Boab, doon fur the day wi' th'wife (a booler frae Fife),
      recoverin' fae
a hert by-pass, 30 years a sergeant in the polis, scrapin'
      deid bodies aff
the road, ex-national serviceman, ex-hun, reprimanded
      last time he was
in for no takin his bunnet aff, fur th'Queen, ex-Labour,
      ex-rabbit-
hutch repairer, is sayin – Blair's War oan Iraq's only fur the
      ile;
the Yanks, ye see, durin' the Vietnam War, some'dy asked
      their President,
Johnson, haw neebs, if th'Arabs turn aff the ile, wull
      America
tak' ower the Middle East? n'Johnson said, the hale place'll
      shut doon
withoot ile, ye ken, an ye cannae hae the hale place shut
      doon
jist cos some cunt wrapt in a sheet says he disnae wantae
      play – he sais;

I gave him away to keep *The Memoir of Sgt Bourgogne*, 1812:
      Napoleon, Moscow, retreat.

Letter from Bathgate
(to Mr Pepys)

Lords day,
June, 1995

I returned these last five years or so ago to Bathgate,
having my partner and no other servant, no more
than the two of us, my brothers and theirs, and my
mother up the road, a balm in Gilead to us all;
my partner, having no absence of terms, gives no hopes
of being with child, which is a little disappointment.

The condition of the State is thus:
Secretary Lang is with his army in Scotland,
and my Lord Major has yet come out of Parliament
to challenge the Rump of the Right in his own Faction,
of whom my Lord Vulcan is their sword bearer,
having been at the House door demanding Entrance,
but Exit also, from Europe, and the curse of a Single
Currency; but it is denied them, and it is believed
that they nor the People will be satisfied till the
House be filled with Merchant Bankers, on all sides.

My private condition rather middling, neither esteemed
rich nor very poor, besides the goods of my house,
which is jointly mortgaged with my partner, and my
office, a bureaucracy of the Social Works, which at
present is uncertain, with the coming of a Common
Council and all the clamour it will much cry up,
and myself all in dirt about the building of my house,
an extension.

And as to this, my purpose, let it be thus:
that I should consider, in the temper of these days,
my own best quality, setting down, in all good order
and conscience, the untidy events of the world,
and for these right reasons: all the people of Fauldhouse;
turtles in the land; the scratch of pens on time.

The Cheap Bean Queue

My father died leaving my mother with five sons grown, a
    budgie, a job she'd
just given up to look after him, an interest in bingo, and a
    turn of phrase
that would start a row in an empty house, or so he'd said,
    like the time Big Betty McFee
remarked at a morning gathering that she could fair jump
    into that cup of tea,
and my mother said, sotto voce – '*Some Cup*!' – well,
    we'd have been as well
opening the coffin and throwing her in as well; anyway,
    as she would say,

she went through a long period of grief, but my young
    brother, who was still
in the house, got her through it, as she did herself, of
    course, but the thing
that got him most was the day she came back all excited
    about getting 'a bargain',
seven battered tins of beans from the Friday market,
    'seven', she said, 'and all half-price';
she wasn't telling him this, of course, but who she'd seen
    while she was standing
in the queue. 'Whit?' he said – 'Did you say you were
    standing in th' cheap bean queue?'

Never one to lie, she said, 'Ay', then he said, 'Mother',
    then, 'Oor Mother',
he said, 'standing in the cheap bean queue, in the middle
    of Bathgate Market?'
'Why Mother?', he said, 'when you've got more money
    than a horse can shite?'
His mother, 'Oor Mother', that is, wasn't exactly sure
    what the point of all this was,
but that was nothing new in this house, so she answered
    straight out, the only way she
knew, 'I like the company', she said, 'I like the company
    of the cheap bean queue.'

The Five Sisters
(Elegy for Shale)

frae the black isles and the borders
twa centuries ago
they laboured roond the calders
above grund and ablo'
and there was no idle bread

O thir faithers they wir bastards and
thir grandfaithers they say
and ivry man a mason grand
no godless Irish they, o no
but I still remember them

mair braw nor a' the Pharoahs
and a' thir chariats hors
and burnished by the burning blaes
but who shall sing for these
the slaves of ancient Egypt?

O ye dochters o' Jerusalem
raise up yir voices sing
men gethered fire in thir airms
t'wrocht cathedrals for thir kings

wherefore,
                let this be thir sepulchre

                till ye hear yir ain skulls crack
                or stare up till the Sisters
                until they stare richt back
                and intil the image o' god

this bit o grund
(transcribed from tom leonard)

choose a piece o grund

> no more than a foot square
> its yours between now and noon
> get doon and look at it
> and just keep lookin at it

there's a lot worse things than falling asleep in a field

> when you move away from it that piece o grund
> wont be noticed
> that's the bit of reality you've got to relate to
> it wont be there tomorrow
>   or maybe this afternoon

that bit o grund has its own importance
> describe it look at it listen to it
> be with and in this piece o grund
> just notice the wee things
>   there

it has its own significance

Football

Flood-lit

Nobody tells you about the lights, how a ball travelling
      towards you,
from gloom to glare, now you see it, now you don't,
      fascinates;
how the dark beyond the arc of light makes the park a
      stage and
tighter than a midge's arse in a sandstorm; nobody tells
      you how the pitch
comes up to meet you like a lift, and the grass flickers
      round your throat;
how the crowd casts up long shadows of the dead in whose
      garb you are,
their coliseum roar, part gynaecological-probe, part divorce-
      lawyer,
giving you the thumbs up, but hoping you'll get nailed
      by a tiger;
nobody tells you how you're stood in the middle of a
      motorway
with everything speeded up, only you're in slow-mo, a
      spectator at your own accident.

Fitba' Cliché
(the ba's no for eatin)

I remember being told by Big MacIntyre
tae take mair time oan the ba'. Listen son, he says,
yer playin like the gress wis oan fire.
Yer blindin us a' wi' the stour.

This is a gemm fur men,
no boays, or weans, or jessies.
If yer good enough, yer big enough, they say,
but, never listen or play tae the crowd,
an' forget a' yer faither's advice,
an' yer great uncle Tam's an a',
wha' played wi' Champfleurie Violet's Cup Winning Team.
They days are a' gaun, like snaw aff
a Geordie Young clearance.

Then
it was the people's gemm,
a' aboot the ba', an beatin' yer men,
this way then that, then swingin it ower frae the wing,
an up like a bird tae heid it awa' an intae the net.
The goalie, auld as yer faither an dressed like yer grannie,
stuck in the mud like a big stranded whale, Goal!
And a hundred thousand voices sang in Hampden Park.
Ye couldnae see the sun fur bunnets.

Romantic?
Ay, and a' for the glory o' it.
Well, that's a' shite noo son,
the ba's no for eatin oanie mair.

Time was
when ye could tell a prospect
by the way he shed his hair,
or jouked by his relations in the scullery,
but we still believed in Empire then,
ken,
when the Wee Blue Devils buried themsels at the England end
and half o' Europe, for a glory that wisnae worth haen,
oor ain, singin an deein like cattle,
brought hame not one lullaby in gaelic.

> In the room the punters come and go
> Talking of Di Stephano

On the terraces,
beneath the stand,
a poet speaks for a nation:

> the ref's a baam.

We,
whaur the comic and the cosmic meet,
an ambulance ball, a crowded street,
a psyche and a jersey steeped ower dark
b'the ruck, a people still, unique,
post modern, post Gramsci (sic),
manoeuvrin, multiform, an chic, ay missus,
chic as fuck.

SCOT-LAND!   SCOT-LAND!   SCOT-LAND!

Scotland,
turn yer backs tae the grandstand,
forget the suicide ba',
think mair o' keepin possession,
(Christ, frae some o yer ain side ana').

Listen.
Ye cannae play fitba' withoot the ba', okay?
An ye cannae govern yerself withoot a country,
even if ye are oan the committee.
(England taught us that)

Right then.

Play yer ain gemm.
Afore the ba' eats us.

Again.

Playing the First Team

Whoosh! Crash! the coke bottle whizzed past Bobby
        Duncan's left foot,
and smashed to smithereens against the pipes beneath the
        benches in Hibernian FC's
dressing-room, Big MacNamee swearing; the reserves
        had just beat
the First Team; at stake a crate of coke for the winners;
        Bob Shankley disappeared,
the floor covered in glass from the bottle Big Mac kicked
        on entering;
sixth in the league, the boss was feart to drop him, even
        though he'd
spend the last ten minutes of every game playing centre;
        the old players
ran the team: some, brilliant, nearing the end, wouldn't
        give you a smell

of their fart, or a pass, to bring the young ones in; but
        Stanton, different class,
a gentleman from Niddrie, took you aside, showed you how to
        head and everything;
Willie Hamilton's in our team, on a comeback between Hibs
        and Hearts and
wherever else he's been, coming round, wearing a rubber
        diving-suit,
towels, two tracksuits on, and built like a skelf, apart from
        the gut;
too tired to run, he'd hit a ball forty-two yards from the
        centre-circle into
the net; came in, stript off, and enough sweat poured out
        to re-float the Titanic;
they said Jock Stein slept with him every Friday night so's
        he'd be ready for the match.

Dirty Tackle
(Brother Grim)

Big Vince just pointed with his chin, and we all just
      looked away, as my older brother, Grim,
broke up the rhythm of their play; an accident, perhaps,
      or a mishap, something stray,
and one of theirs would soon be off, or limping on the
      wing, getting medical attention
or booked for conduct unbecoming; then Vince would
      quietly say, 'weel done Jim',
still on the field of play, and never a hint of sin or guilt to
      cloud the Saturday of one
who'd head small wingers on the neck while jumping for
      the ball, then claim the ricochet
a shy while they were on their backs; for that was only
      fun, a joke, nothing meant,
nothing that involved a crack, a knee left in, something
      stiff and sore and lingering,

not even 'ye'll be takin' yer ba's hame in a barra', for he
      rarely swore, and only warned,
when he didn't need to war or hassle, if the points could
      be secured by other means;
they played us on the right, me just in front of him, the
      theory was, they said,
he'd never kick his kin, but they stuck a big Red-Cross
      where my number should have been,
just in case. Just in case what? Well, take Big Bandy Blair,
      Broxburn, who'd lumbered from the back,
a desperate run astride the ball, a granite block on dodgy
      knees, who wouldn't stop, so I just
nudges him and dives away: three ribs broke, Bandy's
      bealing, and Grim, carrying the stretcher.

Bag-men

Men screamed at Baillie's callused hands, breeze blocks
      rubbing on winter-green,
like having hot-ash massaged into thighs, rough as a
      badger's-arse; 'Jock', they'd say,
'do me first', handing him the liniment, as Baillie came
      between – 'I'll do that, son'.
In twelve seasons, never saw a sponge; a towel and cold
      water in an old lemonade bottle
was all there was, and the threat of them all that was
      needed to have players going down
with broken toes, or a ruptured spleen, spring to their feet
      and wave Jock Philiban away,
and his side-kick, old Baillie, clambering from the dug-out
      – 'It's all right, Jock',
you'd say. 'Where's it hurt son?', but you knew, whether it
      was your eyes or nose or
constipation, as you were saying it, you'd hear a glug, and
      feel your left boot filling up
with cold water, and Baillie rubbing your balls; you'd
      stagger back to your position,
more dazed, with a water-logged foot and an erection; the
      towels round their necks
were for ornament, public display, like the drapes they put
      round coffins at funerals.

Committee Men

They'd gather by pie-stands, a huddle of coats, twenty or
      more, like gambling-schools,
the chill air, the grounds deserted, the crowds still
      finishing their pints, laying bets, still
wondering whether to go or not; the secretaries reading
      out players' names for the vote,
a roll call of the undead; the goalies first, most hands
      raised, then the backs, then
the half-back lines, for this was back in time, before the
      coaches came, guys who'd played
the game, not these, fans who sold raffle-tickets, put nets
      up, ran the lines,
hero-worshipped from afar, or maligned, those whose
      boots they might lace but never fill.

Players hung about outside dressing-rooms watching this
      semaphore, like waiting for the smoke
to clear after some papal death; jokes cracked but eyes
      cast heaven-ward, and stares,
anxious or resigned, confident or brash, wondering what
      the score was: would they
be played today? their fate in numpty hands that knew
      not what the difference was between
a big ball and a wee one, but always wanted grandstand
      when caution was the game,
who favoured showy bastards who could talk but always
      ran from pain and responsibility,
who'd set you up then act outraged when every ball they
      gave you was a grave-yard.

'Give them their place', Big Vince'd say, the first player-
    coach in Junior Scotland's ranks,
which meant he'd let them rave & rant every Wednesday
    after training then pick the one's he'd want;
guys freed by the more fashionable clubs, who'd been
    displaced by arse-lickers,
local boys or the president's son, who they'd then gub
    when 4:2:4 was still considered alchemy;
Ginger ran the line, our curse, the only honest flagman in
    the league 'Remember, Ginger,'
Vince'd say, 'one way! And only us!': and as we left the
    dressing-room, Ginger, the game's last
romantic, knew he'd be in for more of this, and worse,
    come half-time, come the oranges.

Playing Left-Back

Wee Murphy, neat as a cat's tongue, moving the table-
      mats about after the game,
like a conjurer with black curly hair; he'd walk over the
      Pentlands from Penicuik to
Pumpherston before the match, a ten mile warm up;
      'always push them out, son,
never in, or we're fucked; show them the wing – they can
      graze out there all they like,
it's where they belong' – the wingers, he'd mean, whose
      downfall he'd plot, then re-play;
'the faster they are, the more you stand back; if they
      cross, well, that's for the centre-half
to head them away, but if they cut through, then it's your
      fau't, son, but you've the pace,
you could give them five yards and catch them in ten; you
      don't even need to kick them,
but do it anyway, it'll keep your eye in'; he was a master
      in his own domain, but cross
the half-way line and his conviction went, as if taking on
      a full-back on the overlap
meant turning into a winger, like committing incest
      against his own kind; at corner-kicks,
he'd trap the foot of guys at the near post, who'd try to
      jump, then flap about like shot doos.

Men in a Suitcase
(a Junior Football dressing-room)

A Wednesday evening in May and the park's brick hard, a
      bottom of the table clash,
and the ball's bouncing two foot higher than you'd want,
      and you're struggling for players;
Jock King's brung in Shug Wylie, an old fashioned centre-
      half, and a warrior, no half measures
and a scaffolder to trade – no like Jock's other coup –
      Man in a Suit Case – a wee guy
fae Shotts, who just wanders in and crashes doon his
      valise upon the trainer's bench,
a huge thing, like an Indian Sikh would bring round the
      doors and sell you ties and pyjamas frae.

He opens the lid and we all keek in, and lo, a pair of
      round-toed boots his father wore,
with bits of skin and bone still clinging from where dad
      had last put the boot in;
Jock puts him on the wing, but that's another story;
      Shug's no teeth, an unfortunate thing,
but the patter's goin' strong and, of course, Shug joins in;
      trouble wi' the wife – what's new?
'But I'll tell you this, she'll no be oot the nicht,' cos I've
      got her teeth here',
and, sure enough, he's holding up her dentures, and hands
      them round; what a game he had tho'.

Tom McNiven's Training
(Hibs & Scotland trainer)

In jungle-green tracksuits like GIs were wearing in
      Vietnam, Tam taught us
a different kind of war: it's not all about power, but
      change of pace, direction,
movement, flow; your body must know what to expect;
      change of pace,
not one-speed, circling the track like a milk-float –
      explode, relax, canter,
skip, reach for the sky, then drop like a stone like you've
      been kicked
in the goolies, and always keep moving; so, up on you're
      toes and canter,
not too fast, just flex your muscles and shake it all loose,
      breath in through your nose –

hold, then blow out hard through your mouth, like you're
      growling at the girl-friend's
badger, it'll give her pleasure and develop your lungs,
      you'll stay down longer than
a nuclear sub, keep moving; when I say left foot, balance
      and stretch out your
right-leg behind you and hold it like Nuryeve would, he's
      a dancer, two, three –
keep running, same pace, turn, run, thumbs up, point
      them forward, your feet will follow;
skiff the grass with your right hand, jump, head the ball
      left, roll,
keep moving; Nureyev, right foot, up, jump, head,
      keep breathing

Mid-field

He took it on the run, leant out, came back in, then let it
      roll between his feet,
a mother hen, nudging her chick's cheek with the outside
      of her boot, looking up, not down,
the ball a part of him, unafraid, the crowd still braying
      for his blood, ingrates,
for he was playing straight and true, right thro' the ball
      and man, and they'd loved him,
till he done their one in, now limping badly on the wing,
      an innocent who'd strayed
too far in, too late, for he'd just kneed him in the face
      while divin' out the way,
then stood on him while talking to the ref: *Ye shouldnae*
      be playin' wi' a leg like that,
he'd said, and the youngster grinned, for he could have
      gotten worse; so he takes
the kick that's touched straight back to him, then surveys
      the field of play:
three guys shouting for a ball Jim Baxter couldnae gi'e
      when he was at his best.

You're Going to the Hibs

Bob Shankley and Eddie Turnbull came to the house,
      different nights, same week,
and spoke to my father in the living-room while I sat in
      the kitchen with my mother,
drinking tea; sixteen years old, twelve-and-a-half-stone,
      five-foot-ten in stocking-soles,
power and pace, a decent long-pass, and an eye for
      reading the game; I thought I'd suit
Aberdeen better than Edinburgh's ball-players, but when
      the old man announced –
'you're going to the Hibs, and the Juniors' (war by other
      means)' to toughen you up' –

well, what did I know, the Beatles were No 1; £4 a week
      and the same again in expenses
(Aberdeen offered £2, enough to pay my keep), and I'd
      train at Easter Road every Tuesday/
Thursday evenings, and school holidays (I was going for
      my highers); they wanted me
full-time, but my father said it was a dicey-game; 'look at
      Alan Cousins', he says,
a teacher through the week who kicked a ball about for
      gain – Homer in tackety-boots –
now that appealed to me, reading T S Eliot on the team-
      bus while the rest played brag;

every Tuesday-Thursday an omlette for tea then a bus to
      Easter Road; strips,
pants, socks stacked in piles, take your pick, then look for
      a pair of gutties
that would fit and maybe not stink like a Turkish taxi-
      driver's loin-cloth; footballing

icons walked past naked, getting treatment, pulling your
      chain, maybe joining in the
ball-games and you'd see how it was done close-up; future
      stars made you realise
you were ordinary, a good club-pro for fifteen years, bar
      injury, if you were lucky;

a pub or a sales job and arthritis at the end of it; nae
      sentiment, no, no in this game,
they'd say, a market-place, where men were bought-and-
      sold like slaves, then 'freed'.

5-a-sides
(Sports Centre, Wednesday, 7 o'clock)

Twang! Hammy's ham-string goes again as he's taking aff
      his jaicket; Wee Rab,
stripped to the waist, Bathgate's Little Buddah; four big
      cheeks, two quick feet
and no much hair left, but a great player nonetheless; ex-
      Dunfermline, excessive
in onythin' frae eatin pies tae drinkin' tae fightin' weemin
      aff, ay, Rab, in yer
dreams; Wee Jock, a human dynamo; Mojo, on a go-slow;
      the Flying Finn, ah, here's a trick,
nah, hear that click? – his knee's gaun, and he's gaun
      doon himsel', in instalments;
Kevin 'the ba's mine' Duggan; Colin, an enigma, a riddle
      of the Sphinx, sometimes
brilliant, sometimes stinks, mince combined with grace;
      Airthur, a heid-case,
always complainin' aboot the kitty and him no gettin'
      oany, but a major singer;
Wee Tam, a whizz-bang, for whom fitba' is wan lang
      whang, an endless skid;
and then there's the kid, Big Eamon himsel', from Dublin,
      which is where his tackles
begin; Eck Mathieson, gone but not forgiven; Big Tam, a
      cultured left-foot, if things
are going great, but can vibrate if you're no pulling your
      own weight; Faggot,
a mistake, broke his leg tripping ower his ain feet; and
      then there's masel',
ah well, the bringer of the ball, ex-Hibee, ex-mair clubs
      than Jack Nicholas,

fifty if I'm a day, and goin' doon in instalments like a' the
      rest, especially
when Sudsie's on yer case – ah, Sudsie, what can you say?
      – Sudzie's just,
Sudzie's just, Sudzie's just, ah well, wi' Sudzie, ye see,
      words just fail.

Big Vince

These were the days when behemoths still stood in the
      tunnel waiting for each other,
to settle things, if one got sent off; Big Vince was built
      like John Charles was,
only bigger; he got to the Scottish Junior Cup Final with
      Pumpherston in 1958,
then First Division with Dundee United; a mining-
      engineer, he became a corporate manager
at Honeywell, flew the Atlantic to talk to flat-tops about
      computers and how to penetrate
Europe, between training sessions at Pumpherston,
      drawing diagrams for guys
who could play, but couldnae spell their own names right;
      he read everything

by Bertrand Russell, biographies of JFK, believed in the
      American Way of Positive Thinking,
and was fascinated by moon-shots; the best coaches of the
      day, Stein, Ramsay and,
of course, Alison, tripped off his tongue – 'ye cannae play
      fitba' withoot the ba',
son', he'd say, and, 'off-side's pish, done'; I'd watched him
      from the terraces
while still a halfling, seen the monstrous Alex Wilson take
      a leap at his chin at a corner
and miss, and when Wilson fell to earth, Vince just fell on
      him, and the ground trembled;
Wilson was stretchered off and the ref didn't even speak
      to Vincent Halpin,

who'd sway like a tower once every match in the middle
       of our penalty box taking, by his way,
the striker on a moon-walk, round the ball, holding him
       off, on a 360 degree run round the
outside, and a life-time if you were in our defence, your
       heart in your mouth, your ring
narrowing to the size and texture of a zoob-zoob, an
       Iceberg toying with the Titanic,
until Vince completed his turn and sent a perfect 45-yard
       pass to a forward who,
transfixed, let the ball run under his foot: going onto the
       park at Pumpherston was like
following Captain Kirk onto the *Spaceship Enterprise*,
       a journey into the unknown.

The Boot Room

The boot room, beneath the stand, the gloom, a cludgie
    wi' no air in; the apprentice stares
and glares at more odd pairs than Mr & Mrs Markos had
    dubbin for and, yes, he has to clean them all,
the whole fucking mess; scrub them, rub them, make
    them, well, fresh; remove the laces,
do the studs, put his hand in where there's been some'dy
    else's toes, nails, bits of skin,
bits of haggis, christ, a human fuckin' foetus, this no
    grim, and he's no even touched Big Ollie's
yet, the cobbler of the team, ball-breaker, welly merchant,
    giver out of gutty and of pain;
how does he get so much blood into the stitching, and
    little bits of brain?

The Steelyard: 1977
(A Pre-Thatcherite Enterprise Zone)

Round midnight, after the waves of bingo players have
      exited from the Pavilion,
in a crowd of cars, buses, cigarette smoke, disappointment
      and waiting husbands,
and after the chip-shop and last train home brigades have
      come and gone,
and the fourteen year old youths, driven by glue, lager
      and metabolic hormonal vibrations
have squared up to each other and been moved on by the
      police, comes my wee brother,
Graemy, and his pal, Davy Post, the well-known Powder-
      hall sprinter, still looking for a party
to gatecrash, for it was Saturday, almost, and *mair drink!*
      mair drink! is screaming through
their veins, when – *Nirvana!* – a cairrie-oot, sitting on its
      own, in the middle of the Steelyard,
a brown paper poke and nobody aboot; Graemy just has
      the can up to his lips when – *wham!*
this boy, who'd been orderin' a taxi to Whitburn, comes
      stormin oot o' a phone-box,
leaps ten foot through the air and plants his foot on
      Graemy's balls, catches the can gracefully,
as Graemy falls, and resumes his phone call, all in the
      time it took Postie, the well-flown
Powderhall sprinter, to reach Whiteside, and switch onto
      the end of Match of the Day.

Digs, Discos & Damsels

Back-streets, cobbles, the Potteries, and my mate's playing
    in the English League,
lower division, on a good Cup run; I'm down training,
    and they're talking short-term
contracts; he's lodging wi' Ena Sharples' gran, and the
    scum on the tomato soup's bobbing
round like World War II deep-water mines, cricket balls
    with spikes on, but he's oblivious,
for we're disco-bound and lookin for a lumber; we down
    Bicardi & Cokes and Lager,
then he pulls us a right pair of goers who think we're two
    superstars – take my pick,
but he fancies the wee thing, black-hair and kind of flat,
    which leaves me Gina Lollabrigida.

She's a looker, what's the catch? Nothin, cos I'm his pal;
    we clatter in through the back
yard and creep up stairs that would have bairned Hilary
    and Ten Sing (later,
he tells me the old dear's deaf's a post, the bastard!); I'm
    in one room,
he's in the other, and pretty soon his bird's calling for her
    mother and I'm about
to put it in when she says she's just sixteen-n-still a virgin,
    never mind,
then she asks me if I love her; fuckin hell! Paris in revolt,
    and I'm givin her a lecture
about guys like me and him, and his head-board's batterin
    the plaster off the ceilin.

Bonnybridge

The grave-yard shift, Bonnybridge Juniors away; Cairns,
    the Connels and their maw,
Ruby – secretary, treasurer, president, washer of strips
    and, if they needed players,
she'd have more children; dispenser of justice and chief
    breaker-in in a land where
breaking-in was reckoned part of the game; they broke-in
    sometimes before it even started;
the fence round the park was needed to keep the crowd
    out; referees prayed,
and locked themselves in the dressing-room afterwards till
    just about closing time,
then dash for hame; the visiting team's team-bus was
    covered in green, or worse;
the injured lay where they fell, till the smell brought the
    cops round, then armistice.

Captain Morgan
(The Road to Wembley)

The road to Wembley looked like all London would have,
    locked, barred
and deserted if Bonnie Prince Charlie's ragged-arsed
    army hadn't
turned back at Derby in 1745, but there was one old
    wine-seller
had stayed open, you know, a right old London vintner,
    with the apron on
and everything, and 300 thirsty Scotsmen wanting to
    buy his liquor,
and maybe hoping for a lick at his daughter, if she was
    willing, but, anyway,

the place was packed to bursting, so Dougie decides to
    send him up
to the benmaist shelf for a bottle of Captain Morgan's
    Best Bay Rum & Ginger,
his latest craving; so the old-guy's crawling up this
    ancient ladder,
and he's breathing through his erse, so Dougie shouts
    up, in a bid
to ease the tension – *And Ur Ye An Auld Sea-Dog Yurself
    Sur?* – well,
the place just explodes, an Dougie's been 'Captain Morgan'
    ever since.

Some other books published by **LUATH** PRESS

Shale Voices

Alistair Findlay
foreword by Tam Dalyell MP
ISBN 0 946487 63 4 PBK £10.99
ISBN 0 946487 78 2 HBK £17.99

'He was at Addiewell oil works. Anyone goes in there is there for keeps.'
JOE, Electrician

'There's shale from here to Ayr, you see.'
DICK, a Drawer

'The way I describe it is, you're a coal miner and I'm a shale miner. You're a tramp and I'm a toff.'
HARRY, a Drawer

'There were sixteen or eighteen Simpsons...
...She was having one every dividend we would say.' SISTERS, from Broxburn

Shale Voices offers a fascinating insight into shale mining, an industry that employed generations of Scots, had an impact on the social, political and cultural history of Scotland and gave birth to today's large oil companies. Author Alistair Findlay was born in the shale mining village of Winchburgh and is the fourth son of a shale miner, Bob Findlay, who became editor of the West Lothian Courier. Shale Voices combines oral history, local journalism and family history. The generations of communities involved in shale mining provide, in their own words, a unique documentation of the industry and its cultural and political impact.

Photographs, drawings, poetry and short stories make this a thought provoking and entertaining account. It is as much a joy to dip into and feast the eyes on as to read from cover to cover.

'Alistair Findlay has added a basic source material to the study of Scottish history that is invaluable and will be of great benefit to future generations. Scotland owes him a debt of gratitude for undertaking this work.'
TAM DALYELL MP

'...lovingly evoked ...isn't an idle intellectual exercise ...laid out in poetic form, captures the music of speech ...love & respect shines through in this book ...one of the finest pieces of social history I've ever read.'
MARK STEVEN, THE SCOTTISH CONNECTION, BBC RADIO SCOTLAND

'...for thousands of people across the country their attitudes, lifestyles and opinions have been formed through an industry which was once the envy of the world ...captures the essence of the feelings of the time.'
LINDSAY GOULD, WEST LOTHIAN COURIER

'...the mighty shale bings of West Lothian seem to be a secret which remarkably few outsiders share. How beautifully their russet grit glows in dawn or evening light.'
ANGUS CALDER, THE SCOTSMAN

'Findlay records their voices, as sharp and red as the rock they worked ...their voices are also, in a strange way, freed. Findlay, himself a poet, lays them out on the page as poetry to capture the 'dynamics of conversation'. The result is to recreate the directness, simplicity and power of everyday speech.'
JOHN FOSTER, THE MORNING STAR

'...the real and rounded history of the people ...important, informative, captivating and inspiring, speckled with hardship and humour, it is well worth a read.'
JOHN STEVENSON, SCOTLAND IN UNISON

'...the class solidarity and sense of sharing with neighbours in good times and bad could enhance the world of today. Alistair Findlay says it much better than I can... do you not feel echoes of Lewis Grassic Gibbon's Sunset Song in this man's writing?'
WILLIAM WOLFE, SCOTS INDEPENDENT

POETRY

Bad Ass Raindrop
Kokumo Rocks
ISBN 1 84282 018 4 PB £6.99

Caledonian Cramboclink: verse, broadsheets and in conversation
William Neill
ISBN 0 946487 53 7 PB £8.99

Men and Beasts: wild men & tame animals
Val Gillies & Rebecca Marr
ISBN 0 946487 92 8 PB £15.00

The Luath Burns Companion
John Cairney
ISBN 1 84282 000 1 PB £10.00

Scots Poems to be read aloud
introduced Stuart McHardy
ISBN 0 946487 81 2 PB £5.00

Poems to be read aloud
introduced by Tom Atkinson
ISBN 0 946487 00 6 PB £5.00

Picking Brambles and Other Poems
Des Dillon
ISBN 1 84282 021 4 PB £6.99

Kate o Shanter's Tale and Other Poems
Matthew Fitt
ISBN 1 84282 028 1 PB £6.99

FICTION

The Road Dance
John MacKay
ISBN 1 84282 024 9 PB £9.99

Milk Treading
Nick Smith
ISBN 0 946487 75 8 PB £9.99

The Strange Case of RL Stevenson
Richard Woodhead
ISBN 0 946487 86 3 HB £16.99

But n Ben A-Go-Go
Matthew Fitt
ISBN 1 84282 014 1 PB £6.99
ISBN 0 946487 82 0 HB £10.99

Grave Robbers
Robin Mitchell
ISBN 0 946487 72 3 PB £7.99

The Bannockburn Years
William Scott
ISBN 0 946487 34 0 PB £7.95

The Great Melnikov
Hugh MacLachlan
ISBN 0 946487 42 1 PB £7.95

The Fundamentals of New Caledonia
David Nicol
ISBN 0 946487 93 6 HB £16.99

LANGUAGE

Luath Scots Language Learner [Book]
L Colin Wilson
ISBN 0 946487 91 X PB £9.99

Luath Scots Language Learner [Double Audio CD Set]
L Colin Wilson
ISBN 1 84282 026 5 CD £16.99

SPORT

Ski & Snowboard Scotland
Hilary Parke
ISBN 0 946487 35 9 PB £6.99

Over the Top with the Tartan Army
Andy McArthur
ISBN 0 946487 45 6 PB £7.99

HISTORY

Civil Warrior
Robin Bell
ISBN 1 84282 013 3 HB £10.99

A Passion for Scotland
David R Ross
ISBN 1 84282 019 2 PB £5.99

Reportage Scotland: History in the Making
Louise Yeoman
ISBN 0 946487 61 8 PB £9.99

Blind Harry's Wallace
Hamilton of Gilbertfield
introduced by Elspeth King
illustrations by Owain Kirby
ISBN 0 946487 33 2 PB £8.99

SOCIAL HISTORY

Pumpherston: the story of a shale oil village
Sybil Cavanagh
ISBN 1 84282 011 7 HB £17.99
ISBN 1 84282 015 X PB £7.99

A Word for Scotland
Jack Campbell
ISBN 0 946487 48 0 PB £12.99

NATURAL WORLD

The Hydro Boys: pioneers of renewable energy
Emma Wood
ISBN 1 84282 016 8 HB £16.99

Wild Scotland
James McCarthy
photographs by Laurie Campbell
ISBN 0 946487 37 5 PB £8.99

Wild Lives: Otters – On the Swirl of the Tide
Bridget MacCaskill
ISBN 0 946487 67 7 PB £9.99

Wild Lives: Foxes – The Blood is Wild
Bridget MacCaskill
ISBN 0 946487 71 5 PB £9.99

Scotland – Land & People: An Inhabited Solitude
James McCarthy
ISBN 0 946487 57 X PB £7.99

The Highland Geology Trail
John L Roberts
ISBN 0 946487 36 7 PB £4.99

'Nothing but Heather!'
Gerry Cambridge
ISBN 0 946487 49 9 PB £15.00

Red Sky at Night
John Barrington
ISBN 0 946487 60 X PB £8.99

Listen to the Trees
Don MacCaskill
ISBN 0 946487 65 0 PB £9.99

THE QUEST FOR

The Quest for the Celtic Key
Karen Ralls-MacLeod and
Ian Robertson
ISBN 0 946487 73 1 HB £18.99

The Quest for Arthur
Stuart McHardy
ISBN 1 842820 12 5 HB £16.99

The Quest for the Nine Maidens
Stuart McHardy
ISBN 0 946487 66 9 HB £16.99

ISLANDS

The Islands that Roofed the World: Easdale, Belnahua, Luing & Seil
Mary Withall
ISBN 0 946487 76 6 PB £4.99

Rum: Nature's Island
Magnus Magnusson
ISBN 0 946487 32 4 PB £7.95

Luath Press Limited

committed to publishing well written books worth reading

LUATH PRESS takes its name from Robert Burns, whose little collie Luath (*Gael.*, swift or nimble) tripped up Jean Armour at a wedding and gave him the chance to speak to the woman who was to be his wife and the abiding love of his life. Burns called one of *The Twa Dogs* Luath after Cuchullin's hunting dog in *Ossian's Fingal*. Luath Press was established in 1981 in the heart of Burns country, and is now based a few steps up the road from Burns' first lodgings on Edinburgh's Royal Mile.
Luath offers you distinctive writing with a hint of unexpected pleasures.

Most bookshops either carry our books in stock or can order them for you. To order direct from us, please send a £sterling cheque, postal order, international money order or your credit card details (number, address of cardholder and expiry date) to us at the address below. Please add post and packing as follows: UK – £1.00 per delivery address; overseas surface mail – £2.50 per delivery address; overseas airmail – £3.50 for the first book to each delivery address, plus £1.00 for each additional book by airmail to the same address. If your order is a gift, we will happily enclose your card or message at no extra charge.

Luath Press Limited
543/2 Castlehill
The Royal Mile
Edinburgh EH1 2ND
Scotland
Telephone: 0131 225 4326 (24 hours)
Fax: 0131 225 4324
email: gavin.macdougall@luath.co.uk
Website: www.luath.co.uk